CHRISTMAS COOKIES

CHRISTMAS COOKIES

MAKE, BAKE AND DECORATE YOUR OWN COOKIES THIS CHRISTMAS

First published in 2013
LOVE FOOD is an imprint of Parragon Books Ltd

Parragon Inc.
440 Park Avenue South, 13th Floor
New York, NY 10016

www.parragon.com/lovefood

ISBN: 978-1-4723-1937-1

Printed in China

Introduction by Linda Doeser
New recipes written by Sandra Baddeley
Internal design by Donna-Marie Scrase
Additional photography by Clive Streeter with food styling by Angela Drake
Cover photography by Mike Cooper

Notes for the Reader
This book uses standard kitchen measuring spoons and cups. All spoon and cup measurements are level unless otherwise indicated. Unless otherwise stated, milk is assumed to be whole, butter is assumed to be salted, and eggs are large.

Garnishes and serving suggestions are all optional and not necessarily included in the recipe ingredients or method. The times given are only an approximate guide. Preparation times differ according to the techniques used by different people and the cooking times may also vary from those given. Optional ingredients, variations, or serving suggestions have not been included in the calculations.

Recipes using raw or very lightly cooked eggs should be avoided by infants, the elderly, pregnant women, and people with weakened immune systems. Pregnant and breast-feeding women are advised to avoid eating peanuts and peanut products. People with nut allergies should be aware that some of the prepared ingredients used in the recipes in this book may contain nuts. Always check the packaging before use.

CONTENTS

INTRODUCTION

For centuries delicious edible treats have been as integral to traditional Christmas celebrations as a kiss beneath the mistletoe. In the week leading up to the great day generations have rolled up their sleeves and bustled about their kitchens baking—cakes particularly, but also breads, pastries, and cookies.

Every country has its own culinary traditions. In France, for example, village children would go from house to house singing carols on Christmas Eve and were rewarded with cornmeal wafers, while warmer spices featured in the cookies from further north— Dutch *speculaas*, German *Lebkuchen*, Swedish *pepparkakor*, and British gingerbread men.

However, it is in the United States where the tradition of baking Christmas cookies has grown and flourished. European immigrants took their Christmas recipes across the Atlantic with them and a new seasonal custom took root. Starting with the invention of the sugar cookie in Pennsylvania, American cooks have developed a vast array of tasty Christmas treats to give as gifts, to offer visiting friends, family, and neighbors, to hang on the Christmas tree, and, of course, to accompany a glass of milk left out for Santa on Christmas Eve.

A SEASONAL TOUCH

Cookies with a Christmas theme are easy to make and decorate. If you make a dough that can be rolled out, you can cut out any number of seasonal shapes. A huge range of specially shaped cookie cutters is available and these will always be popular with children.

You don't have to be particularly artistic to decorate Christmas-themed cookies. It's a wonderful pre-Christmas activity to share with excited children and even preschoolers can drizzle frosting and sprinkle colored sugar with a surprising degree of accuracy.

Once cookies are frosted, a good supply of colored and chocolate sprinkles, gold and silver balls, sugar shapes, such as stars and flowers, edible glitter, and even small candies can be applied immediately and will keep children happily, if slightly messily, occupied for half an hour. Almost as easy is decorating with colored sugar. Mix superfine sugar with a little food coloring paste in a plastic bag, rubbing it well in, then sprinkle over unset frosting or on a topping of melted chocolate.

Piped frosting decorations always look special but do take a little practice and a fairly steady hand. Cookies are a good place to begin, since they are small, easy to handle, and a homemade quality only adds to their charm. Food-coloring pens can sometimes be a

7

good alternative to piping. Available in a wide range of colors, these look like felt-tip pens and can be used to decorate dry, firm frosting. They are ideal for writing names, initials, and messages on cookies, drawing designs such as stripes, spots, and stars, and for coloring in shapes.

CHRISTMAS COOKIE SWAP

If you've never taken part in a cookie swap, and you're an ardent cookie lover, you don't know what you've been missing! It's a fantastic opportunity to share tasty treats and well-tested recipes with friends and family, and to discover a great selection of home-baked goodies that you're sure to make again and again.

Whether you're a seasoned swapper or new to the world of the cookie exchange, a few simple rules will make sure you have a smooth event every time:

• Calculate how many guests you plan to invite; consider friends, family, and neighbors—it's a great social event!
• Specify that all cookies must be homemade and baked; many established swaps stipulate no chocolate-chip cookies, no-bakes, meringues, or bars, but you should decide what suits your guests' level of baking expertise.
• Consider how many cookies each swapper will need to bake and, equally, how many each guest will be able to take home.
• Send invitations! If you're planning your cookie swap far in advance, you should also send a save-the-date card.
• Always ask for an RSVP to your invitations, and remember to ask what each guest is baking, so that you can be sure there's no repetition.
• Remind guests to bring suitable containers for transporting their cookies home at the end of the swap.

Baking cookies is creative, enjoyable, and simple—it is a great way to create something really delicious in a short space of time. Get your invitations in the mail and let the fun begin!

PERSONALIZE YOUR BAKING

Throughout this book you will see recipes marked with this *Stamp Me* icon (shown below)—these cookies are suitable for use with the alphabet cookie stamp. Before use, remember to wash the letters and holder in warm soapy water, then rinse and dry thoroughly. Separate the letters and cut away the connecting tabs with scissors. Then load your message into the holder—remember that the letters must go into the holder backwards, in order to leave the impression the right way around on the cookie itself. Dip the stamp in flour and tap off the excess—this will prevent it from sticking in the cookie dough. Once the dough has been rolled, cut, and positioned on the baking sheet, press the stamp into the dough, using an even pressure to leave a clear impression. Bake the cookies as directed. Wash the stamp in warm soapy water and again, rinse and dry thoroughly before storing for use another day.

Snowflake
GINGERBREAD

Makes 30

- 3 cups all-purpose flour, plus extra for dusting
- 1 tablespoon ground ginger
- 1 teaspoon baking soda
- ¾ stick plus 1 tablespoon butter, softened, plus extra for greasing
- heaping ¾ cup brown sugar
- 1 egg, beaten
- 4 tablespoons light corn syrup

To decorate

- 1 cup confectioners' sugar
- 2 tablespoons lemon juice

1 Preheat the oven to 350°F. Grease three cookie sheets.

2 Sift the flour, ginger, and baking soda together into a bowl. Add the butter and rub into the flour until the mixture resembles fine breadcrumbs, then stir in the brown sugar.

3 In another bowl, beat together the egg and light corn syrup with a fork. Pour this mixture into the flour mixture and mix to make a smooth dough, kneading lightly with your hands.

4 Roll out the dough on a lightly floured surface to about ¼ inch/5 mm thick and cut into shapes using a snowflake-shaped cutter. Transfer the cookies to the prepared cookie sheets.

5 Bake in the preheated oven for 10 minutes, until golden brown. Let cool for 5 minutes before transferring to a wire rack to cool completely.

6 Once the cookies are cool, combine the confectioners' sugar and lemon juice until smooth and spoon into a pastry bag fitted with a fine tip. Pipe snowflake shapes onto each cookie with the icing. Let set for a few hours.

Eggnog
COOKIES

Makes 35

- 1 egg
- heaping ¾ cup superfine sugar
- 6 tablespoons rum
- 3 tablespoons milk
- 1¼ stick plus 1 tablespoon butter, softened, plus extra for greasing
- 1 teaspoon vanilla extract
- 2 egg yolks
- 2½ cups all-purpose flour
- 1 teaspoon baking powder
- ¾ teaspoon ground nutmeg
- 1½ cups confectioners' sugar

1 Preheat the oven to 325°F. Grease two cookie sheets. To make the eggnog mixture, beat together the egg, 2 tablespoons of the superfine sugar, the rum, and milk until frothy. Set aside.

2 In a large bowl, beat together the rest of the superfine sugar and all but 1 tablespoon of the butter until light and fluffy. Beat in the vanilla extract and egg yolks until smooth.

3 Sift together the flour, baking powder, and ½ teaspoon of the nutmeg into the mixture and beat in ½ cup of the eggnog mixture until just combined.

4 Place heaping teaspoonfuls of the mixture on the prepared cookie sheets, spaced well apart. Flatten slightly with damp fingers and bake in the preheated oven for 20–25 minutes, until the bottoms of the cookies turn golden. Let cool for 5 minutes on the cookie sheets and then transfer to a wire rack to cool completely.

5 Once the cookies are cool, beat together the confectioners' sugar, remaining butter, and the remaining eggnog mixture to make a soft frosting. Spread the frosting over the cookies and sprinkle with a little nutmeg on top. Let set for a few hours.

Spiced
RUM COOKIES

Makes 18
- 1 ½ sticks unsalted butter, plus extra for greasing
- 1 cup dark brown sugar
- 2 cups all-purpose flour
- pinch of salt
- ½ teaspoon baking soda
- 1 teaspoon ground cinnamon
- ½ teaspoon ground coriander
- ½ teaspoon ground nutmeg
- ¼ teaspoon ground cloves
- 2 tablespoons dark rum

1 Preheat the oven to 350°F. Grease two cookie sheets.

2 Cream together the butter and sugar and whisk until light and fluffy. Sift the flour, salt, baking soda, cinnamon, coriander, nutmeg, and cloves into the creamed mixture.

3 Pour the dark rum into the creamed mixture and stir well. Place small mounds of the mixture onto the prepared cookie sheets. Flatten each one slightly with the back of a spoon.

4 Bake in the preheated oven for 10–12 minutes, or until golden. Let the cookies cool and become crisp on wire racks before serving.

Santa
SUGAR COOKIES

Makes 40

- 3 cups all-purpose flour, plus extra for dusting
- 1 teaspoon baking powder
- ¼ teaspoon salt
- 1 stick butter, softened, plus extra for greasing
- heaping ¾ cup superfine sugar
- 1 egg, beaten
- 2½ teaspoon vanilla extract
- 1 tablespoon milk

To decorate
- 2 cups confectioners' sugar
- 1 egg white
- ½ teaspoon glycerin
- glycerin-based red and black food coloring

1 Grease four cookie sheets. Sift the flour, baking powder, and salt together into a bowl. In a separate bowl, beat the butter and superfine sugar together until light and fluffy. Beat in the egg, 2 teaspoons of the vanilla extract, and the milk until smooth and then mix in the flour mixture to form a soft dough. Cover the dough with plastic wrap and chill in the refrigerator for 30 minutes.

2 Preheat the oven to 350°F. Roll out the chilled dough on a lightly floured surface to ¼ inch/5 mm thick. Use a Santa-shaped cutter to cut out shapes from the dough. Transfer the cookies to the prepared cookie sheets. Bake in the preheated oven for 10 minutes, until golden brown. Remove from the oven and let cool for 5 minutes before transferring to a wire rack to cool completely.

3 Once the cookies are cool, beat together the confectioners' sugar, egg white, remaining vanilla extract, and glycerin with an electric mixer for 5 minutes, until stiff and glossy. Color one-third of the confectioners' sugar mixture red and color 2 tablespoons of the mixture black. Leave the rest of the mixture as white icing. Apply the red icing evenly with a small spatula to create Santa's hat, and pipe eyes in black icing using a fine nozzle. Put the white icing into a pastry bag fitted with a small star-shaped tip to create the fur trim, eyebrows, moustache, and pom-pom on Santa's hat. Apply the remainder of the icing, using a swirling action, with a small spatula to create his beard. Let set for a few hours.

Reindeer
COOKIES

Makes 25

- 10 cardamom pods
- ¾ stick plus 2 tablespoon butter, softened, plus extra for greasing
- ¼ cup superfine sugar
- 1 egg, beaten
- finely grated rind of ½ orange
- 2 cups all-purpose flour, plus extra for dusting
- ¼ cup cornstarch
- ½ teaspoon baking powder

To decorate

- heaping ¾ cup confectioners' sugar
- 4 teaspoons lemon juice
- glycerin-based red food coloring
- 25 edible silver balls

1 Crush the cardamom pods lightly in a pestle with a mortar and discard the shells. Grind the cardamom seeds to a powder. Beat together the butter and superfine sugar in a bowl with a whisk until creamy, then gradually beat in the egg, orange rind, and cardamom powder.

2 Sift together the flour, cornstarch, and baking powder into the mixture and stir with a wooden spoon to form a soft dough. Wrap the dough in plastic wrap and chill in the refrigerator for 30 minutes.

3 Preheat the oven to 350°F. Grease three cookie sheets. Roll out the chilled dough on a lightly floured surface to ⅛ inch/3 mm thick. Cut out shapes using a reindeer-shaped cutter and place on the prepared cookie sheets. Knead and reroll the trimmings and cut out more shapes until all the dough is used up.

4 Bake in the preheated oven for 15 minutes, until just golden. Let cool for 5 minutes before transferring to a wire rack to cool completely. Combine the confectioners' sugar and lemon juice until smooth. Spoon 2 tablespoons of the mixture into a separate mixing bowl and color it with the red food coloring.

5 Spoon the rest of the icing into a pastry bag fitted with a fine tip and pipe antlers, hooves, a tail, collar, and a saddle in white icing on each cookie. Pipe a nose using the red icing. For the eye, attach a silver ball using a blob of icing.

Cinnamon & Chocolate
CHIP COOKIES

Makes 30

- 2 sticks butter, softened
- scant ¾ cup superfine sugar
- 1 egg yolk, lightly beaten
- 2 teaspoons orange extract
- 2½ cups all-purpose flour
- pinch of salt
- heaping ½ cup semisweet chocolate chips

Cinnamon coating
- 1½ tablespoons superfine sugar
- 1½ tablespoons ground cinnamon

1 Preheat the oven to 375°F. Line two cookie sheets with parchment paper.

2 Put the butter and sugar into a bowl and mix well with a wooden spoon, then beat in the egg yolk and orange extract. Sift together the flour and salt into the mixture, add the chocolate chips, and stir until thoroughly combined.

3 For the coating, mix together the sugar and cinnamon in a shallow dish. Scoop out tablespoons of the cookie dough, roll them into balls, then roll them in the cinnamon mixture to coat. Flatten the cookies slightly with your fingers and put them on the prepared cookie sheets, spaced well apart.

4 Bake in the preheated oven for 12–15 minutes. Let cool on the cookie sheets for 5–10 minutes, then transfer to wire racks to cool completely.

Cranberry & Coconut
COOKIES

Makes 30

- 2 sticks butter, softened
- scant ¾ cup superfine sugar
- 1 egg yolk, lightly beaten
- 2 teaspoons vanilla extract
- 2½ cups all-purpose flour
- pinch of salt
- ½ cup unsweetened
  dried coconut
- ½ cup dried cranberries

1 Preheat the oven to 375°F. Line two cookie sheets with parchment paper.

2 Put the butter and sugar into a bowl and mix well with a wooden spoon, then beat in the egg yolk and vanilla extract. Sift together the flour and salt into the mixture, add the coconut and cranberries, and stir until thoroughly combined. Scoop up tablespoons of the dough and place in mounds on the prepared cookie sheets, spaced well apart.

3 Bake in the preheated oven for 12–15 minutes, until golden brown. Let cool on the cookie sheets for 5–10 minutes, then transfer to wire racks to cool completely.

Cookie
CANDY CANES

Makes 40

- 3 cups all-purpose flour, plus extra for dusting
- 1 teaspoon baking soda
- ¾ stick plus 1 tablespoon butter, softened, plus extra for greasing
- heaping ¾ cup brown sugar
- 1 egg, beaten
- 1 teaspoon vanilla extract
- 4 tablespoons light corn syrup

To decorate
- 4 cups confectioners' sugar
- generous ½ cup lemon juice
- glycerin-based red food coloring

1 Preheat the oven to 350°F. Grease three cookie sheets.

2 Sift the flour and baking soda together into a bowl. Add the butter and rub into the flour until the mixture resembles fine bread crumbs, then stir in the brown sugar. In another bowl, beat together the egg, vanilla extract, and light corn syrup with a fork. Pour this mixture into the flour blend and stir to make a smooth dough, kneading lightly with your hands.

3 Roll out the dough on a lightly floured surface to about ¼ inch/5 mm thick and cut into shapes using a candy cane-shaped cutter. Transfer the cookies to the prepared cookie sheets. Bake in the preheated oven for 10 minutes, until golden brown. Remove the cookies from the oven and let cool for 5 minutes before transferring to a wire rack to cool completely.

4 Once the cookies are cool, combine 2½ cups of the confectioners' sugar and 5 tablespoons of lemon juice until smooth. Spoon the mixture into a pastry bag fitted with a fine tip and pipe the icing around the edge of the cookies. Empty any remaining icing into a small bowl, color it with the red food coloring, and cover with plastic wrap.

5 Combine the remaining confectioners' sugar and remaining lemon juice until smooth and runny. Spoon this into the center of each cookie and spread to the piped edge to flood each cookie. Let set overnight, then spoon the red icing into a pastry bag fitted with a fine tip and pipe stripes, dots, and swirls over the dry iced cookies.

Apple &
SPICE COOKIES

Makes 30

- 2 sticks butter, softened
- scant ¾ cup superfine sugar
- 1 egg yolk, lightly beaten
- 2 teaspoons apple juice
- 2½ cups all-purpose flour
- ½ teaspoon ground cinnamon
- ½ teaspoon apple pie spice
- pinch of salt
- ½ cup finely chopped dried apple, soaked overnight

Apple filling

- 1 tablespoon superfine sugar
- 1 tablespoon vanilla pudding mix
- ½ cup milk
- 5 tablespoons applesauce

1 Put the butter and sugar into a bowl and mix well with a wooden spoon, then beat in the egg yolk and apple juice. Sift together the flour, cinnamon, apple pie spice, and salt into the mixture, add the dried apple, and stir until thoroughly combined. Halve the dough, shape into balls, wrap in plastic wrap, and chill in the refrigerator for 30–60 minutes.

2 Preheat the oven to 375°F. Line two cookie sheets with parchment paper.

3 Unwrap the dough and roll out between two sheets of parchment paper. Stamp out cookies with a 2-inch/5-cm square cutter and put them on the prepared cookie sheets, spaced well apart. Bake in the preheated oven for 10–15 minutes, until light golden brown. Let cool on the cookie sheets for 5–10 minutes, then transfer to wire racks to cool completely.

4 To make the filling, combine the sugar, pudding mix, and milk in a saucepan and bring to a boil, stirring continuously. Cook, stirring continuously, until thickened, then remove the saucepan from the heat and stir in the applesauce. Cover the surface with plastic wrap and let cool.

5 Spread the filling over half of the cookies and top with the remaining halves.

Christmas
BELLS

Makes 30

- 2 sticks butter, softened
- scant ¾ cup superfine sugar
- finely grated rind of 1 lemon
- 1 egg yolk, lightly beaten
- 2½ cups all-purpose flour
- ½ teaspoon ground cinnamon
- pinch of salt
- heaping ½ cup semisweet chocolate chips

To decorate

- 2 tablespoons lightly beaten egg white
- 2 tablespoons lemon juice
- 2 cups confectioners' sugar
- 30 edible silver balls
- food-coloring pens

1 Put the butter, superfine sugar, and lemon rind into a bowl and mix well with a wooden spoon, then beat in the egg yolk. Sift together the flour, cinnamon, and salt into the mixture, add the chocolate chips, and stir until thoroughly combined. Halve the dough, shape into balls, wrap in plastic wrap, and chill in the refrigerator for 30–60 minutes.

2 Preheat the oven to 375°F. Line two cookie sheets with parchment paper.

3 Unwrap the dough and roll out between two sheets of parchment paper. Stamp out cookies with a 2-inch/5-cm bell-shaped cutter and put them on the prepared cookie sheets, spaced well apart.

4 Bake in the preheated oven for 10–15 minutes, until light golden brown. Let cool on the cookie sheets for 5–10 minutes, then transfer to wire racks to cool completely.

5 Combine the egg white and lemon juice in a bowl, then gradually beat in the confectioners' sugar until smooth. With the cookies still on the racks, spread the icing over them. Place a silver ball on the clapper shape at the bottom of the cookie and let set completely. When the icing is dry, use the food-coloring pens to draw patterns on each cookie.

Cinnamon
STARS

Makes 20

- 2 egg whites
- 1½ cups confectioners' sugar, plus extra for dusting
- 2¼ cups roasted ground hazelnuts
- 1 tablespoon ground cinnamon

1 Whisk the egg whites in a clean, dry bowl until stiff. Stir in the sugar until thoroughly combined, then continue to whisk until thick and glossy.

2 Remove one-sixth of this mixture and set aside. Then fold in the hazelnuts and cinnamon into the remaining mixture to make a very stiff dough. Chill in the refrigerator for about 1 hour.

3 Preheat the oven to 275°F. Line two cookie sheets with parchment paper. Roll out the dough to ½ inch/1 cm thick on a counter generously dusted with confectioners' sugar.

4 Cut the dough into shapes using a 2-inch/5-cm star-shaped cutter, dusting with confectioners' sugar in between to prevent it from sticking. Reroll as necessary until all the mixture is used up.

5 Place the cookies on the prepared cookie sheets, spaced well apart, and spread the top of each star with the reserved egg-white icing.

6 Bake in the preheated oven for 25 minutes, until the cookies are still white and crisp on top but slightly soft and moist underneath. Turn off the oven and open the oven door to release the heat and dry out the cookies in the oven for 10 more minutes. Transfer to wire racks to cool.

Blueberry, Cranberry & Cinnamon
COOKIES

Makes 30
- 2 sticks butter, softened
- scant ¾ cup superfine sugar
- 1 egg yolk, lightly beaten
- 2 teaspoons vanilla extract
- 2½ cups all-purpose flour
- 1 teaspoon ground cinnamon
- pinch of salt
- ½ cup dried blueberries
- ½ cup dried cranberries
- ½ cup pine nuts, chopped

1 Preheat the oven to 375°F. Line two cookie sheets with parchment paper.

2 Put the butter and sugar into a bowl and mix well with a wooden spoon, then beat in the egg yolk and vanilla extract. Sift together the flour, cinnamon, and salt into the mixture, add the blueberries and cranberries, and stir until thoroughly combined.

3 Spread out the pine nuts in a shallow dish. Scoop up tablespoons of the mixture and roll them into balls. Roll the balls in the pine nuts to coat, then place on the prepared cookie sheets, spaced well apart, and flatten slightly.

4 Bake in the preheated oven for 10–15 minutes. Let cool on the cookie sheets for 5–10 minutes, then transfer the cookies to wire racks to cool completely.

Walnut & Fig
PINWHEELS

Makes 30

- 2 sticks butter, softened
- 1 cup superfine sugar
- 1 egg yolk, lightly beaten
- 2 cups all-purpose flour
- pinch of salt
- ½ cup ground walnuts
- 1⅔ cups dried figs, finely chopped
- 5 tablespoon freshly brewed mint tea
- 2 teaspoons finely chopped fresh mint

1 Put the butter and ¾ cup of the sugar into a bowl and mix well with a wooden spoon, then beat in the egg yolk. Sift together the flour and salt into the mixture, add the ground walnuts, and stir until thoroughly combined. Shape the dough into a ball, wrap in plastic wrap, and chill in the refrigerator for 30–60 minutes.

2 Meanwhile, put the remaining sugar into a saucepan and stir in ½ cup of water, then add the figs, mint tea, and chopped mint. Bring to a boil, stirring continuously, until the sugar has dissolved, then lower the heat and simmer gently, stirring occasionally, for 5 minutes. Remove the saucepan from the heat and let cool.

3 Unwrap the dough and roll out between two sheets of parchment paper into a 12-inch/30-cm square. Spread the fig filling evenly over the dough, then roll up like a jelly roll. Wrap in plastic wrap and chill in the refrigerator for 30 minutes.

4 Preheat the oven to 375°F. Line two cookie sheets with parchment paper.

5 Unwrap the roll and cut into thin slices. Put the slices on the prepared cookie sheets, spaced well apart. Bake in the preheated oven for 10–15 minutes, until golden brown. Let cool on the cookie sheets for 5–10 minutes, then transfer to wire racks to cool completely.

Christmas
TREE COOKIES

Makes 12

- heaping 1 cup all-purpose flour, plus extra for dusting
- 1 teaspoon ground cinnamon
- ½ teaspoon ground nutmeg
- ½ teaspoon ground ginger
- 5 tablespoons unsalted butter, diced, plus extra for greasing
- 3 tablespoons honey

To decorate
- white icing (optional)
- edible colored balls (optional)

1 Sift the flour and spices into a bowl and rub in the butter until the mixture resembles breadcrumbs. Add the honey and mix together well to form a soft dough. Wrap the dough in plastic wrap and chill in the refrigerator for 30 minutes.

2 Meanwhile, preheat the oven to 350°F and grease two cookie sheets. Divide the dough in half. Roll out one piece of dough on a floured surface to about ¼ inch/5 mm thick. Cut out tree shapes using a cutter or cardboard template. Repeat with the remaining piece of dough.

3 Put the cookies on the prepared cookie sheets and, using a toothpick, make a hole through the top of each cookie large enough to thread a ribbon through. Chill in the refrigerator for 15 minutes.

4 Bake in the preheated oven for 10–12 minutes, until golden. Let cool on the cookie sheets for 5 minutes, then transfer to a wire rack to cool completely. Decorate the trees with white icing and colored balls, or simply leave them plain, then thread a length of ribbon through each hole and knot. Hang from the Christmas tree.

Stained-glass Window
COOKIES

Makes 25

- 2¾ cups all-purpose flour, plus extra for dusting
- pinch of salt
- 1 teaspoon baking soda
- ¾ stick plus 1 tablespoon unsalted butter, diced
- scant 1 cup superfine sugar
- 1 extra large egg
- 1 teaspoon vanilla extract
- 4 tablespoon light corn syrup
- 9 ounces mixed colored hard fruit candies

1 Sift the flour, salt, and baking soda into a large bowl, add the butter, and rub it in until the mixture resembles breadcrumbs. Stir in the sugar. Place the egg, vanilla extract, and corn syrup in a separate bowl and whisk together. Pour the egg into the flour mixture and mix to form a smooth dough. Wrap in plastic wrap and chill in the refrigerator for 30 minutes.

2 Preheat the oven to 350°F. Line two large cookie sheets with parchment paper. Roll the dough out on a floured work surface to ¼ inch/5 mm thick. Use a variety of floured cookie cutters to cut out the cookies. Transfer them to the cookie sheets and cut out shapes from the center of the cookies. Using a skewer, make a hole in the top of each cookie.

3 Unwrap the candies and sort into separate bowls by color. Lightly crush the candies by tapping them with a rolling pin. Fill the holes in the centers of the cookies with the crushed candies.

4 Bake in the preheated oven for 10–12 minutes, or until the candies are melted. Make sure the holes are still there, and pierce again if necessary. Let cool on the cookie sheets until the centers have hardened. When cold, thread thin ribbon through the holes to hang up the cookies.

Spiced
FRUIT COOKIES

Makes 30

- 2 sticks butter, softened
- scant 3¾ cup superfine sugar
- 1 egg yolk, lightly beaten
- 2½ cups all-purpose flour
- ½ teaspoon apple pie spice
- pinch of salt
- ¼ cup chopped plumped
  dried apple
- ¼ cup chopped plumped
  dried pear
- ¼ cup chopped plumped
  dried plum
- grated rind of 1 orange

1 Put the butter and sugar into a bowl and mix well with a wooden spoon, then beat in the egg yolk. Sift together the flour, apple pie spice, and salt into the mixture, add the apple, pear, plum, and orange rind, and stir until thoroughly combined. Shape the dough into a log, wrap in plastic wrap, and chill in the refrigerator for 30–60 minutes.

2 Preheat the oven to 375°F. Line two cookie sheets with parchment paper.

3 Unwrap the log and cut it into ¼-inch/5-mm thick slices with a sharp serrated knife. Put them on the prepared cookie sheets, spaced well apart.

4 Bake in the preheated oven for 10–15 minutes, until golden brown. Let cool on the cookie sheets for 5–10 minutes, then transfer the cookies to wire racks to cool completely.

GINGERSNAPS

Makes 30

- 2½ cups self-rising flour
- pinch of salt
- 1 cup superfine sugar
- 1 tablespoon ground ginger
- 1 teaspoon baking soda
- 1 stick plus 1 tablespoon butter, plus extra for greasing
- ¼ cup light corn syrup
- 1 egg, lightly beaten
- 1 teaspoon grated orange rind

1 Preheat the oven to 325°F. Grease two cookie sheets.

2 Sift together the flour, salt, sugar, ground ginger, and baking soda into a large mixing bowl.

3 Heat the butter and corn syrup together in a saucepan over very low heat until the butter has melted. Let the butter mixture cool slightly, then pour it onto the dry ingredients. Add the egg and orange rind and mix together thoroughly.

4 Using your hands, carefully shape the dough into 30 even-sized balls. Place the balls on the prepared cookie sheets, spaced well apart, and flatten slightly with your fingers.

5 Bake in the preheated oven for 15–20 minutes. Carefully transfer the cookies to a wire rack to cool completely.

Christmas Tree
DECORATIONS

Makes 20

- 2 sticks butter, softened
- scant ¾ cup superfine sugar
- 1 egg yolk, lightly beaten
- 2 teaspoons vanilla extract
- 2½ cups all-purpose flour
- pinch of salt
- 1 egg white, lightly beaten
- 2 tablespoons colored sprinkles
- 14 ounces mixed colored hard fruit candies

1 Put the butter and sugar into a bowl and mix, then beat in the egg yolk and vanilla extract. Sift together the flour and salt into the mixture and stir until thoroughly combined. Halve the dough, shape into balls, wrap in plastic wrap, and chill in the refrigerator for 30–60 minutes.

2 Preheat the oven to 375°F. Line two cookie sheets with parchment paper.

3 Unwrap the dough and roll it out between two sheets of parchment paper. Stamp out cookies with Christmas-themed cutters and put them on the prepared cookie sheets, spaced well apart. Stamp out rounds from each shape and remove them. Make a small hole in the top of each cookie with a skewer so that they can be threaded with ribbon. Brush with egg white and decorate with the sprinkles. Bake in the preheated oven for 7 minutes.

4 Meanwhile, unwrap the candies and sort into separate bowls by color. Lightly crush the candies by tapping them with a rolling pin. Remove the cookies from the oven and fill the holes with the crushed candies. Return to the oven and bake for an additional 5–8 minutes, until the cookies are light golden brown and the candies have melted and filled the holes. If the holes for hanging the cookies have closed up, pierce them again with the skewer while the cookies are still warm. Let cool completely on the cookie sheets. Thread ribbon through and hang.

Holly
LEAF COOKIES

Makes 30
- 4 tablespoons butter, softened, plus extra for greasing
- scant ½ cup superfine sugar
- 1 egg yolk
- ⅛ teaspoon almond extract
- 1 cup all-purpose flour, plus extra for dusting
- 2 teaspoons milk
- 3 ounces mixed colored hard fruit candies

1 Beat the butter and sugar together in a bowl until light and fluffy. Beat in the egg yolk and almond extract until smooth and then sift in the flour and add the milk to produce a soft dough. Cover with plastic wrap and chill in the refrigerator for 30 minutes.

2 Preheat the oven to 350°F. Grease two cookie sheets. Crush the candies in their wrappers with a rolling pin. Roll out the chilled dough on a lightly floured counter to ¼ inch/5 mm thick.

3 Use a large holly leaf-shaped cutter to cut out shapes from the dough and then use a smaller holly-shaped cutter to cut out and remove the middle of each larger holly shape.

4 Place all the holly shapes on the prepared cookie sheets. Using a toothpick, cut a small hole out of the top of each cookie so they can be threaded with ribbon. Repeat until all the dough is used up.

5 Divide the crushed hard candy pieces evenly to fill the holes in the middle of the cookies. Bake in the preheated oven for 8–10 minutes, until the cookies are just turning golden around the edges.

6 When completely cool, transfer the cookies to a wire rack. Thread thin ribbons through the holes and hang from the branches of the Christmas tree.

Iced
STARS

Makes 30

- 2 sticks butter, softened
- ¾ cup superfine sugar
- 1 egg yolk, lightly beaten
- ½ teaspoon vanilla extract
- 2 cups all-purpose flour
- pinch of salt

To decorate

- 1¾ cups confectioners' sugar
- 1–2 tablespoons warm water
- food colorings
- edible silver and gold balls
- colored sprinkles
- edible sugar stars, hearts, and flowers
- dry unsweetened coconut

1 Place the butter and superfine sugar in a large bowl and beat together until light and fluffy, then beat in the egg yolk and vanilla extract. Sift together the flour and salt into the mixture and stir until thoroughly combined. Halve the dough, shape into balls, wrap in plastic wrap, and chill in the refrigerator for 30–60 minutes.

2 Preheat the oven to 375°F. Line two large cookie sheets with parchment paper.

3 Unwrap the dough and roll out between two sheets of parchment paper to about ⅛ inch/3 mm thick. Cut out cookies with a star-shaped cutter and place them on the prepared cookie sheets, spaced well apart. Bake in the preheated oven for 10–15 minutes, or until light golden brown. Let cool on the cookie sheets for 5–10 minutes, then transfer to wire racks to cool completely.

4 To decorate, sift the confectioners' sugar into a bowl and stir in enough warm water until it is the consistency of thick cream. Divide the icing among 3–4 bowls and add a few drops of your chosen food colorings to each. Leave the cookies on the racks and spread the different colored icings over them to the edges. Arrange colored balls on top and/or sprinkle with colored sprinkles and sugar shapes. If you like, color dry unsweetened coconut with food coloring in a contrasting color and sprinkle over the cookies. Let set.

Christmas
GIFT COOKIES

Makes 30

- 2 sticks butter, softened
- ¾ cup superfine sugar
- 1 egg yolk, lightly beaten
- 2 teaspoon orange juice or orange liqueur
- finely grated rind of 1 orange
- 2 cups all-purpose flour
- pinch of salt

To decorate

- 1 egg white
- 2 cups confectioners' sugar
- red and green food coloring
- edible silver balls

1 Place the butter and superfine sugar in a large bowl and beat together until light and fluffy, then beat in the egg yolk, orange juice, and grated rind. Sift together the flour and salt into the mixture and stir until combined. Halve the dough, shape into balls, wrap in plastic wrap, and chill in the refrigerator for 30–60 minutes.

2 Preheat the oven to 375°F. Line two large cookie sheets with parchment paper. Unwrap the dough and roll out to ⅛ inch/3 mm thick. Cut out appropriate shapes, such as stars, with cookie cutters and place them on the cookie sheets, spaced well apart. Bake in the preheated oven for 10–15 minutes, or until light golden brown.

3 Let cool on the cookie sheets for 5–10 minutes, then transfer the cookies to wire racks to cool completely.

4 Leave the cookies on the racks. Place the egg white and confectioners' sugar in a bowl and beat until smooth, adding a little water, if necessary. Transfer half of the icing to another bowl and color each bowl with a different color. Place both icings in pastry bags with fine tips and use to decorate the cookies; write the initials of the person who will receive the cookies as a gift. Finish with silver balls and let set.

Cinnamon &
ORANGE WAFERS

Makes 30

- 2 sticks butter, softened
- 1 cup superfine sugar
- finely grated rind of 1 orange
- 1 egg yolk, lightly beaten
- 4 teaspoons orange juice
- 2 cups all-purpose flour
- pinch of salt
- 2 teaspoons ground cinnamon

1 Place the butter, ¾ cup of the sugar, and the orange rind in a large bowl and beat together until light and fluffy, then beat in the egg yolk and 2 teaspoons of the orange juice. Sift together the flour and salt into the mixture and stir until thoroughly combined. Shape the dough into a ball, wrap in plastic wrap, and chill for 30–60 minutes.

2 Unwrap the dough and roll out between two sheets of parchment paper into a 12-inch/30-cm square. Brush with the remaining orange juice and sprinkle with the remaining sugar and cinnamon. Lightly roll with the rolling pin. Roll up the dough like a jelly roll. Wrap in plastic wrap and chill for 30 minutes.

3 Preheat the oven to 375°F. Line two large cookie sheets with parchment paper.

4 Unwrap the dough and cut into thin slices, then place on the prepared cookie sheets, spaced well apart. Bake in the preheated oven for 10–12 minutes. Let cool for 5–10 minutes, then transfer to wire racks to cool completely.

Christmas
ANGELS

Makes 25

- 2 sticks butter, softened
- scant ¾ cup superfine sugar
- 1 egg yolk, lightly beaten
- 2 teaspoons passion-fruit pulp
- 2½ cups all-purpose flour
- pinch of salt
- ⅔ cup dry unsweetened coconut

To decorate

- 1½ cups confectioners' sugar
- 1–1½ tablespoons passion-fruit pulp
- edible silver glitter, for sprinkling

1 Put the butter and superfine sugar into a bowl and mix well with a wooden spoon, then beat in the egg yolk and passion-fruit pulp. Sift together the flour and salt into the mixture, add the coconut, and stir until thoroughly combined. Halve the dough, shape into balls, wrap in plastic wrap, and chill in the refrigerator for 30–60 minutes.

2 Preheat the oven to 375°F. Line two cookie sheets with parchment paper.

3 Unwrap the dough and roll out between two sheets of parchment paper. Stamp out cookies with a 2¾-inch/7-cm angel-shaped cutter and put them on the prepared cookie sheets, spaced well apart.

4 Bake in the preheated oven for 10–15 minutes, until light golden brown. Let cool on the cookie sheets for 5–10 minutes, then transfer to wire racks to cool completely.

5 Sift the confectioners' sugar into a bowl and stir in the passion-fruit pulp until the icing has the consistency of thick cream. With the cookies still on the racks, spread the icing over them. Sprinkle with the edible glitter and let set.

German
LEBKUCHEN

Makes 60

- 3 eggs
- 1 cup superfine sugar
- heaping ⅓ cup all-purpose flour
- 2 teaspoons unsweetened cocoa
- 1 teaspoon ground cinnamon
- ½ teaspoon ground cardamom
- ¼ teaspoon ground cloves
- ¼ teaspoon ground nutmeg
- 2 cups ground almonds
- ⅓ cup candied peel, finely chopped

To decorate
- 4 ounces semisweet chocolate, broken into pieces
- 4 ounces white chocolate, broken into pieces
- sugar crystals

1 Preheat the oven to 350°F. Line several large cookie sheets with parchment paper. Place the eggs and sugar in a heatproof bowl set over a saucepan of gently simmering water and whisk until thick and foamy. Remove the bowl from the pan and continue to whisk for 2 minutes.

2 Sift the flour, cocoa, cinnamon, cardamom, cloves, and nutmeg into the bowl and stir in the ground almonds and candied peel. Drop heaping teaspoonfuls of the mixture onto the prepared cookie sheets, spreading them gently into smooth mounds.

3 Bake in the preheated oven for 15–20 minutes, or until light brown and slightly soft to the touch. Let cool on the cookie sheets for 10 minutes, then transfer the cookies to wire racks to cool completely.

4 Place the semisweet and white chocolates in two separate heatproof bowls, set the bowls over two pans of gently simmering water, and heat until melted. Dip half of the cookies in the melted semisweet chocolate and half in the white chocolate. Sprinkle with sugar crystals and let set.

Spicy Cinnamon
DRIZZLES

Makes 25

- 1½ sticks plus 2 tablespoons butter, softened
- 2 tablespoons molasses
- scant ¾ cup superfine sugar
- 1 egg yolk, lightly beaten
- 2½ cups all-purpose flour
- 1 teaspoon ground cinnamon
- ½ teaspoon ground nutmeg
- ½ teaspoon ground cloves
- pinch of salt

- 2 tablespoons chopped walnuts

To decorate
- 1 cup confectioners' sugar
- 1 tablespoon hot water
- yellow and pink food coloring

1 Put the butter, molasses, and superfine sugar into a bowl and mix well with a wooden spoon, then beat in the egg yolk. Sift together the flour, cinnamon, nutmeg, cloves, and salt into the mixture, add the walnuts, and stir until thoroughly combined. Halve the dough, shape into balls, wrap in plastic wrap, and chill in the refrigerator for 30–60 minutes.

2 Preheat the oven to 375°F. Line two cookie sheets with parchment paper.

3 Unwrap the dough and roll out between two sheets of parchment paper to about ¼ inch/5 mm thick. Stamp out cookies with a 2½-inch/6-cm fluted cutter and put them on the prepared cookie sheets.

4 Bake in the preheated oven for 10–15 minutes, until firm. Let cool on the cookie sheets for 5–10 minutes, then transfer the cookies to wire racks to cool completely.

5 To decorate, sift the confectioners' sugar into a bowl, then gradually stir in the hot water until the icing has the consistency of thick cream. Spoon half of the icing into another bowl and stir a few drops of yellow food coloring into one bowl and a few drops of pink food coloring into the other. With the cookies still on the racks, using teaspoons, drizzle the yellow icing over them in one direction and the pink icing over them at right angles. Let set.

Silver
STAR COOKIES

Makes 36

- ½ cup all-purpose flour, plus extra for dusting
- 1 teaspoon ground cinnamon
- 1 teaspoon ground ginger
- 6½ tablespoons butter, diced
- scant ½ cup light brown sugar
- finely grated rind of 1 orange
- 1 egg, lightly beaten

To decorate

- 1¾ cups confectioners' sugar
- 3–4 teaspoons cold water
- edible silver cake sprinkles
- edible silver balls

1 Preheat the oven to 350°F. Line several large cookie sheets with parchment paper.

2 Sift the flour, cinnamon, and ginger into a large bowl. Add the butter and rub it in with your fingertips until the mixture resembles fine breadcrumbs. Stir the brown sugar and orange rind into the mixture, add the egg, and mix together to form a soft dough.

3 Roll the dough out thinly to about ¼ inch/5 mm thick on a lightly floured work surface. Cut out shapes with a 2½-inch/6.5-cm star-shaped cutter and place on the prepared cookie sheets.

4 Bake in the preheated oven for 10–15 minutes, or until golden brown. Let cool on the cookie sheets for 2–3 minutes, then transfer the cookies to a wire rack and let cool completely.

5 To make the icing, sift the confectioners' sugar into a large bowl and add enough water to make a smooth icing. Spread a little on each cookie, then decorate with sprinkles and silver balls.

Christmas Stocking
COOKIES

Makes 30

- ¾ stick plus 1 tablespoon butter, plus extra for greasing
- ¼ cup superfine sugar
- 1 egg, beaten
- finely grated rind and juice of 1 lemon
- 2 cups all-purpose flour, plus extra for dusting
- ¼ cup cornstarch, plus extra for dusting
- ½ teaspoon baking powder
- 1 tablespoon apple pie spice

To decorate

- glycerin-based red and green food coloring
- 9 ounces ready-to-use fondant
- 2½ cups confectioners' sugar
- 1 egg white
- ½ teaspoon glycerin

1 Beat together the butter and superfine sugar in a bowl with an electric mixer until creamy. Then beat in the egg and lemon rind. Sift together the flour, cornstarch, baking powder, and spice into the batter and stir to combine thoroughly into a soft dough. Wrap in plastic wrap and chill for 30 minutes.

2 Preheat the oven to 350°F. Grease two cookie sheets. Roll out the dough on a lightly floured counter to ¼ inch/5 mm thick. Using a Christmas stocking-shaped cutter, cut out shapes from the dough and place on the prepared cookie sheets. Knead and reroll the trimmings and cut out shapes until all the dough is used up. Bake in the preheated oven for 15 minutes, until just golden. Let cool for 5 minutes before transferring to a wire rack to cool.

3 Mix the green coloring into 1 ounce of the fondant, adding a little confectioners' sugar, until well blended. Cover to prevent it from drying out. Repeat with remaining fondant and the red food coloring. Roll out the green fondant as thinly as possible on a surface lightly dusted with cornstarch and cut out shapes using a small holly-leaf cutter. Set aside. Roll out the red fondant, again as thinly as possible. Cut out shapes using the Christmas stocking-shaped cutter. Stick each stocking to the cookie by using a little lemon juice. Beat together the remaining confectioners' sugar, the egg white, and glycerin for 5 minutes with an electric mixer until stiff and glossy. Slacken the mixture with a little lemon juice to make it thick, but still possible to pipe. Fill a pastry bag, fitted with a small star-shaped nozzle, with this icing mixture. Pipe rows of stars to form a furry cuff on each stocking. Stick a holly-leaf shape into the piped icing on each cookie.

63